C

FIVE JOAQUINS

Also from the Emma Press:

The Emma Press Anthology of Mildly Erotic Verse
A Poetic Primer for Love and Seduction: Naso Was My Tutor
The Emma Press Anthology of Motherhood
The Emma Press Anthology of Fatherhood

Raspberries for the Ferry, by Andrew Wynn Owen
Ikhda, by Ikhda, by Ikhda Ayuning Maharsi

More Emma Press Picks:

The Flower and the Plough, by Rachel Piercey
The Emmores, by Richard O'Brien
The Held and the Lost, by Kristen Roberts

CAPTAIN LOVE
And the FIVE
JOAQUINS

A TALE OF THE OLD WEST BY JOHN CLEGG

ILLUSTRATED BY EMMA WRIGHT

THE EMMA PRESS

THE EMMA PRESS

First published in Great Britain in 2014
by the Emma Press Ltd

ISBN 978-1-910139-01-1

A CIP catalogue record of this book is
available from the British Library.

Printed and bound in Great Britain
by Letterworks, Reading.

theemmapress.com
editor@theemmapress.com

Z

To my mother

A memento of California
And to remind her never to return

HISTORICAL NOTE

In the summer of 1853, Captain Harrison Love of the California State Rangers travelled through several towns exhibiting a head in a water-jar, which he claimed to have taken from the shoulders of the *bandito* Joaquin Murrieta, leader of the notorious Five Joaquins. This was a lie; Murrieta was still alive. Love, it seems, had assumed that any Mexican head and a compelling story would be enough to claim the $1000 bounty. His state of mind as that story began to fall apart can be imagined; while he was certainly a rash, violent man, he does not give the impression of having been particularly courageous.

The Captain's subsequent career, and the strange way in which he met his end, are well documented; what happened afterwards to Murrieta must remain conjecture. In his own words, '¿Pero cómo sabrán los venideros, entre la niebla, la verdad desnuda?'[citation needed].

Captain Love
detained another fortnight at the Governor's

must send to Fresno
for his dress spurs (bluegold

with enameled rowel and Yellow Rose
motif along the shank in filigree)

and wonders lightly if it would be wise
to place a certain object on the outbound coach

and have it disappear en route? –
his man could surely

sling it in a gully somewhere,
watch it bounce once, whumpf, a spurt of dust –

and when the coach returned
the man would buff the horses in the stableblock

there'd be a quiet word
and later, waiting to collect his pay

he'd feel the icy tickle
of Love's dress sword underneath his chin and Love
        would hold his peace

then press
and tamp the worry down for good.

Love's worry feeds on worry
like the dustdevil that pivots round to eat itself.

It can't be tamped down.
Both stitched eyes are coming open.

With one week left to claim commission Love
rode into town, the jarred head jolting in his
parfleche saddlebag, the head he would 'exhibit to
the curious' on payment of a small administration
charge; he set his stall out in the backroom of the
slightly higher-class saloon and called for water
(for himself) and pure grain alcohol, one gallon
(to preserve the head). The Mayor had crossed
the street in company of two reporters from the
California Police Gazette and withdrew from the
First Great Western Bank ten hundred-dollar bills,
Love's bounty, and the invitation from the Governor
was on the mail coach that evening, and the
California Police Gazette led with the gunfight at
Arroyo de Cantua, and the routing of the outlaw
gang known as the Five Joaquins, and Love's long
ride from mining camp to mining camp, tent city
to tent city, backwater to backwater, bearing for
display the pickled head of Joaquin Murrieta.

That said, unless the alcohol
has healed Murrieta's scar

and blotted his tattoo
that's someone else's head.

Some loose threads where Love's tale
might snag: his vanished cowhand

(lying empty-necked
halfway along Arroyo de Cantua,

ribs a mess of rag and string already);
the coincidence

of bringing down his man
so near the bounty's expiration date;

the lack of witnesses; the testament of Murrieta's sister
who reports Joaquin

alive and well (though much the worse for drink)
a full week after his decapitation.

Then the note:
one morning

on his breakfast-tray
neat copperplate

$500
or I talk

To negotiate the sale of another massive land
tranche, scrub and whitestone, Santa Anna and
his entourage will commandeer the guest-wing of
the hacienda for a weekend. The Governor asked
Captain Love to stay another week and oversee
security, and Love could not refuse, although since
the arrival of the note his worry was a wildfire,
skimming ridge to ridge and menacing whole
redwood stands. The Map Room was prepared,
the zone in question ringed in white thread: gritty
quadrilateral fit for nothing more than driving rail-
roads straight over, Alta California's last mortgaged
edgeland.

The Five Joaquins (now down to four)
hijack a mail coach outside Laredo

whose guard, in a feat
of imbecile bravado, gulps the strongbox key

and swallows.
Powder being scarce, the Joaquins

are obliged to sit with him all night and wait.
They trade tequila-swigs to move his bowels

and make him read aloud
a clipping from the *California Police Gazette*

where one Joaquin thought he'd discerned, yessir,
a likeness in the batch of woodcut mugshots.

And lastly, Murrieta
facedown in a lemon orchard

sleeps two days off three weeks drunk.
He quit the gang to play piano

in a Tijuana cathouse.
When he heard he'd died

he had the bright idea to bum to Fresno
and collect the bounty on himself.

I cut a deal in Guayaquil
For an Inca silver mine, he slurs,

But before they found it was salted ground
I was safe in the Argentine –

Love isn't safe. The lines across his palm, which
Ezmerelda stared at for so long before confessing
she could read no future there, have started to
converge. One eye popped halfway open over-
night and Love was busy with his needle in the
morning. Nothing's ready for the visit. Love must
send to Fresno for his epaulettes.

Dolores won't undress for him
with 'that *thing*' watching her

and Ezmerelda shudders
at the floaty leer of it – as if

the smile was a ballgown trimmed
to flash the merest *hint* of tooth –

and Manuela
leaves Love's balcony unswept;

even his sabre
catches in the scabbard

when he practice-draws it,
like a choked-back word, a hatching yucca moth.

8

He writes as near-illegibly
as he can manage: *Aug.: Ignacio Sigarra of Sonora,*

*being duly sworn, says he has seen the head
and that the head was that of Joaquin Murrieta,*

*celebrated bandit, with whom
the deponent was acquainted –*

one more feint
to throw behind him if needs be.[1]

One more chicane.
His split nib pools ink

in the folds and ridges
in the imperfections of the lie.

Joaquin Botellier, the smartest of the four Joaquins
(now down to three), provides addenda in coyote

---

1 – ... one more fake affidavit
in the Joaquin Murrieta

Wikipedia edit war,
the final rearguard skirmish of Love's lie...

language to the calls which flex and boom above their heads, as all three bandits shiver on their bedrolls. Halfway through the blank plain of Tulare, halfway to the Governor, halfway to Captain Love who claimed the bounty on their names. *Dispersed or dead!* (That said, Joaquin Carillo did disperse, lacking the mettle or the appetite for desert treks. He's off to deal pinochle on a steamboat.) Intermittently (between Botellier's coyote shouts) the three talk tactics:

JOAQUIN: The perimeter, no problem. Two, three guards at most.
JOAQUIN: We masked and all in black.
JOAQUIN: Stake out his outhouse.
JOAQUIN: When he comes up close we grapple him.
JOAQUIN: Like ghosts but warm.
JOAQUIN: At night along the little cobbled path.
JOAQUIN: (coyote hoot)
JOAQUIN: He pay us then the lot. By rights it's ours. Plus more –
JOAQUIN: By morning, or before, our bounty doubles.

He thinks: if he should ditch the head
and doubt crept in,

as now no doubt it must –
the Governor

or some ambitious
corporal in his retinue –

and there the thought
hiccups and gives out.

Small breeze stirs
across the matilija

petals on his windowsill.
Each crumpled linen shirtsleeve hides a gold piastre.

And he thinks: if he should keep the head
and doubt crept in,

as now no doubt it must –
and there the thought

rears up like Skyball Paint the devil's horse
and throws him back –

the head would testify,
the mouth slump open, speak

the name which Love
heard only once ('Señor, please

tell my wife –') and which
had quit him by the time he reached Sonora.

Lightning currycombs the dune flanks, flicks the
whiptail lizard from her den. His Most Serene
Antonio de Padua María Severino López de Santa
Anna is delayed in Magdalena. Love rides hard to
where the second note directed him, dismounts
and waits in pouring rain and no-one shows. His
hand goes to his swordhilt then to grip the fold of
blackmail bills then to adjust his spurs.

Later he shins the cottonwood to reach his balcony
unnoticed, having stowed the horse. Unbuttoning a
sodden shirt he realises – his whole gut plummets
– that the head is missing from the mantelpiece.

At the masked ball
(this was Love's dream)

thrown to welcome Santa Anna,
Love danced twice with Ezmerelda

unencumbered of her sadness,
suddenly promoted

from a kitchenmaid
into a minor noblewoman,

red-dressed,
dominoed –

and then the dream blurred,
Love was seated at high table

where the Governor was speaking. 'Now,
Your Highness, honoured Gentlemen, a toast

to our good Captain here
who last week took a trophy, hem, a trophy

from a certain fugitive
whose outlawry and depredations were a byword once

on both sides of the border:
raise your glasses, gentlemen, to our brave Captain Love!'

Then Santa Anna's waxwork mouth
creaked open, coughed: 'I fought alongside this man Murrieta

at Chapultepec; I should be glad
to see his coward's face again before I die. Please fetch the head.'

The three Joaquins (now down to two) rode into Fresno having eaten nothing for a week but rattlesnake and slabs of cactus flesh. They'd left the sunstruck Joaquin Valenzuela in a dry arroyo, barely conscious: neither had the heart to finish him. (Two Chumash hunters stumble on him later; he recurs in legend as a local ghost, a placename, and the logo of a nearby short-lived vineyard.) Fresno's streets were blistery hexagons of dry mud. In an old saloon the Joaquins planned their spree, they'd seize the Mayor first, as he stumbled to the outhouse from the card-room…

Love wakes up.
His worry flails aimless

round the bed
until it latches

on the new note,
its precise directions –

Ride out to Arroyo de Cantua
where you left the body –

for the first time signed,
a dashed-off Z.

He rises, dresses,
crosses to the stable compound.

Worry's volatile, straining
to resolve into specific fear.

Now Love's so tired
he would take command

from anyone, his horse,
his better instincts,

from the head itself, if he
could hold it, from the tongues

of fire in the eyes –
as he rides past

jackrabbits in the underbrush
stand stockstill, pistol hammers rusted shut.

To ride with Zorro was an honour, Murrieta
thought, to rise before dawn, steal two fresh horses
every day ('Tornado, old friend,' Zorro whispered;

each new horse was Zorro's old Tornado), scrounge
red wine and bedclothes from the garrison.

Never much said. On two occasions righted very
minor local wrongs. Preferred a hard bed, earth if
need be. (Murrieta slept against the slow lift, slow
fall of the latest horse.)

Their path through California seemed almost
random, until Murrieta realised it described a *Z*,
crossbar three hundred miles end to end, and that
its final line would give out in Arroyo de Cantua.
Didn't raise it. And his master wouldn't have responded.

Love finds his old way down
to where creekwater

eddies round the torso
held together

by a rawhide holster,
peels flecks, flows on discoloured.

There's the flat rocklip
that kept his rifle level.

There's the waterfall
whose shallow bristle

flung back sun
like rocksalt from a 12-bore.

Zorro hollers from above the gorge.
Love gets the tone

but not the words.
(Rethinking this scene afterwards,

the sense of something
crucial having slipped his grasp.)

The thrown head
tumbles through the dust

and comes to rest against Love's boot.
The thread gives out.

Both eyes snap open:
Love's impression, seared against each retina.

Murrieta came round. Tunnel, stretching off to
vanishing. Near-total dark at first. The memory
of how Love's terror-yell had spooked the horses,
hoof-stamp, how the gully wall had sheared and

ilt both riders down into the waterfall's plunge pool. So where was this? He noticed how his vision was adjusting faster than seemed normal, like a door was gently opening behind him. Something told him not to look. From out the parting dark stepped Zorro, hands behind the head, not in surrender (Murrieta realised gradually) but to undo the mask. The mask fell free and it was Ezmerelda.

Murrieta said: 'Where are we?'
        Underground.
'What are we doing here?'
        You think that you were born in Hermosillo
        [Murrieta nodded], that your father was a
        mustang catcher, that you have one sister and
        no brother. [Murrieta nodded.]
        None of this is true. You come from El Dorado.
        When you left you drank the water of the sacred
        lake and lost your memory of home. I rode
        and rode to find you.
'Why?'
        Your brothers and yourself are my lost sons.
'Brothers?'
        You have a thousand brothers, all Joaquins.

Joaquin Botellier and Joaquin Ocomorenia stepped out from the dark, clasped hands with Murrieta.

'How did you get here?' asked Murrieta.
Joaquin said: 'A trapdoor in the hoosegow.'
'Tell me once more where we are?'
        This under-road leads back to El Dorado.
        Hidden doors all over California open onto here.

Staring down the tunnel after maybe fifty feet it
seemed pure dark. He tried to make out any glint of
gold. 'How far is it away?' His mother shrugged.
       Much further than you can imagine.
Tied her mask and melted back to darkness.

Some time passed. The brothers started walking.

Captain Love
hurried a makeshift prayer

above the head
rough-wedged in gravel,

pesos, thumb-pressed, weighing down each eyelid.
Then he rode alone into the great cease.

Captain I'll be no more;
>   But I will eat and drink, and sleep as soft
>   As captain shall: simply the thing I am
>   Shall make me live.

– *Much Ado About Nothing* (IV, 3)

ACKNOWLEDGMENTS

I am grateful to Alex Bell, Alex MacDonald, Charlotte Geater, Holly Hopkins, John Canfield and Narayani Menon for advice and discussion, and especially to Emma Wright and Rachel Piercey for their careful editing. Thank you to Eli Lischka for help with the Spanish, and Sarah Clegg for additional research.

ABOUT THE POET

John Clegg's first collection is *Antler* (Salt, 2012). Other poems have been published in *Best British Poetry 2012*, *Best British Poetry 2013*, the *Salt Book of Younger Poets*, and various magazines and anthologies. In 2013 he received an Eric Gregory Award. He lives in London.

ABOUT THE ILLUSTRATOR

Emma Wright studied Classics at Brasenose College, Oxford. She worked in ebook production at Orion Publishing Group before leaving to set up The Emma Press in 2012. In 2013 she toured the UK with 'The Mildly Erotic Poetry Tour', supported with funding from Arts Council England as part of the Lottery-funded Grants for the arts programme.

THE EMMA PRESS

small press, big dreams

The Emma Press is an independent publisher
dedicated to producing books which are sweet, funny and
beautiful. It was founded in 2012 in Winnersh, UK, by Emma
Wright and the first Emma Press book, *The Flower and the
Plough* by Rachel Piercey, was published in January 2013.

Our current publishing programme includes a mixture of
themed poetry anthologies and single-author pamphlets,
with an ongoing engagement with the works of the Roman
poet Ovid. We publish poems and books which excite us,
and we are often on the lookout for new writing to feature
in our latest projects.

Visit our website and sign up to the Emma Press newsletter
to hear about all upcoming calls for submissions as well
as our events and publications. You can also purchase our
other titles and poetry-related stationery in our online shop.

http://theemmapress.com

MORE EMMA PRESS PICKS:

THE HELD AND THE LOST

by Kristen Roberts

ISBN: 978 0 9574596 8 7
Price: £5 / $9

A moving collection of distinctly Australian poems about love, marriage and family life. Kristen Roberts is laid-back but precise as she sketches out sympathetic portraits of characters and relationships against the backdrop of swaying eucalypts, roses and occasional rain. These are love poems with their eyes wide open and scars defiantly on display.

THE EMMORES
by Richard O'Brien

ISBN: 978 0 9574596 4 9
Price: £5 / $9

Richard O'Brien (Foyle Young Poets of the Year Award winner, 2006 and 2007) deploys every trick in the love poet's book in this fascinating pamphlet of poems, written in response to a new long-distance relationship and loosely inspired by the Roman poet Ovid's *Amores*. An irresistible mix of tender odes, introspective sonnets, exuberant free verse and anthems of sexual persuasion.

THE FLOWER AND THE PLOUGH
by Rachel Piercey

ISBN: 978 0 9574596 0 1
Price: £5 / $9

Rachel Piercey (Newdigate Prize, 2008) considers the dynamics of love and relationships in this stunning debut collection. Romantic but never sentimental, Piercey approaches her subject with emotional and linguistic clarity and builds up a nuanced study of passion and heartbreak, capturing everything from the extravagant surrender of early love to the raw ache and pain that can follow.